The Gift of Boats

Acknowledgments

Thanks are due to the editors of publications in which some of these poems made a first appearance: *Magma, Poetry London, Poetry Review, The North, The Rialto, Scintilla, Smiths Knoll* and *Contourlines* (Salt, 2009).

'The Gift of Boats' won the 2009 Academi Cardiff International Poetry Competition.

Also by Jane Routh:

Circumnavigation (Smith/Doorstop, 2002)
Teach Yourself Mapmaking (Smith/Doorstop, 2006)

The Gift of Boats
Jane Routh

Smith/Doorstop Books

Published 2010 by
Smith/Doorstop Books
The Poetry Business
Bank Street Arts
32-40 Bank Street
Sheffield S1 2DS
www.poetrybusiness.co.uk

ISBN 978-1-906613-22-8

British Library Cataloguing-in-Publication Data.
A catalogue record for this book is available from the
British Library.

Typeset by Utter
Printed by Charlesworth, Wakefield
Cover design by Utter
Cover image: Gig, Stern View by James Dodds,
www.jamesdodds.co.uk

Smith/Doorstop Books is a member of Inpress,
www.inpressbooks.co.uk. Distributed by Central Books Ltd.,
99 Wallis Road, London E9 5LN.

The Poetry Business gratefully acknowledges the help of
Arts Council England.

Supported by
ARTS COUNCIL
ENGLAND

CONTENTS

i.m. my mother

THE AFTERLIVES OF BOATS

Better scuttled than filled with earth
and concreted to a square lobelia sea
with waves of white alyssum under the bow
and – in place of mast and shrouds – poles
for runner beans, tall dahlias
where you'd want to see red sails;

though even sunk a boat will surface
in the swill of tides and make for land.
You can always find broken planks
among boulders on the shore, like those
I collected near Auliston Point,
silvered, with raised grain
and streaks of red lead – and all too beautiful
to be of use. I left them to the air.

Better by far bottom-up
and heaved onto low stone walls
so the re-caulked and commodious hull
still shelters, the straight line of her keel
slicing the wind as it once did the Sound,
thwarts where ropes and oars were stored
now roof beams to hang them from
(even her name re-painted the other way up)
and the flare of her beam always catching your eye,
comforting as a familiar constellation
glimpsed over the plunge of a midnight bow.

THE GIFT OF BOATS

A present, you say, fishing out of the blue
carrier bag a small oar, and another,
then four more stowed in a black currach,
futtocks and knees pressing her skins;
next, a lobster boat with warps and pots
and a keep-net on board, a coat of red lead
on her bottom ready for winter
(though the wheelhouse looks fixed
slightly skewiff) and a last handful
of marker buoys with tiny cork floats
flagged blue and green and two in red,
not made from a kit, by a modeller,
but by someone who knew about boats
– their lines and their stemposts and deadwoods –
a man with a gift for a seaworthy boat
whom we reconstruct from his work:
cautious (the extra oars) and precise, a man
who likes to plan ahead (the coloured flags),
well used to boats in rough seas
(those double floats) with big hands
that made his lobsterpots oversized,
a make-do-and-mend man all his life,
always down to the strandline among rocks
after an onshore wind: a few floats,
a mooring linc, a well-varnished hatchboard
just right for his chicken coop door
and a piece of marine ply, an odd shape
but enough for the wheelhouse roof
he's painted white, a man whose own boat
was a salvage job he reclaimed,
with an old Lister engine stripped down
on the kitchen table over winter, saying

he minded the tides and wouldn't need
more than seven knots, she was sound
– like these two up on their cradles
re-glued and made ready for sea,
£3 each from the junk shop, and underpriced.

FORTY FATHOMS OF PIANO WIRE WOUND ROUND A PIECE OF FISHBOX

The companionway's five steps, backwards
into warmth and fumes, eyes not yet making it out
Mind Your Head too late on polished brass
and stronger than the smell of diesel, rubber, paint
or bladderwrack, the smell of breakfast,
mackerel fried in oatmeal with bacon fat, suddenly
just what your body wants, like it wants
up into a short bunk, leecloths laced tight
against the world, only the sway and roll of it
telling who's where and what for – but you know
it never was like that: the past was bitter,
salt-crusted, cut, exhausted.
They knew it too and yet through all of it
– neglect and war, and years of ferrying cement –
preserved her feeling-wire, as if this
were the heart of it, the hands' knowledge
of what had been struck in the depths.

*The best wireman on this stretch of coast was Big Jim
Henderson. He could've worked on newer boats, but wouldn't
leave the 'Lizzie Ann'. They say she never once tore a net when
he was on board. He'd tell you by strikes on the wire what was
in a shoal beside herring. You wouldn't have thought it from the
size of the man – his hands – but he was a fiddler too; always
wanted at a wedding. Past 80 when I knew him: I never heard
him play – arthritis – though they say he'd tune up late at night
when he was on his own. He was a great one for a yarn.*

SABBATH

Boy Andrew, Nil Desperandum and Kestrel,
the Harmony and the Welcome Home
tide-rode at their moorings
under a sky the colour of mussel shells.

Minutes after midnight, a diesel starting up.
That trick with slipping lines;
the luminous bands on an overall
unhurried, to the wheelhouse.

A steaming light. Revs
echoing back off the rocks, then slow
between the channel buoys, then faint.
Onshore, a curtained upstairs light goes out.

RED SKY IN THE MORNING

Flannan Isles Lighthouse, 1900

i
a taper reflected briefly across brilliant lenses
the steady yellow beam
paraffin – the smell of work

a lightkeeper must be a man of parts, a handyman
a useful cook and a good companion
at peace with himself and with the world

the clockwork *like clockwork*
chains smooth and easy, slow
revolution of the light

the beam, its double flare, count 30
the beam, its double flare
the beam

to keep watch at night
to ensure light flash correctly to character
to keep a fog watch

the beam, its double flare
catching spume on Soray
       spume on Soray

sea like ink
seabirds screaming in with the dark
a job with much loneliness and isolation its composition

offshore (if anyone is there to see)
you can make out only
a far-off loom across the night sky

loom across the night sky
             the night sky
                      sky

                      sky paling, grey

ii
clouds rolling east,
reddening as the sun comes up
then sliding shut

barometer and thermometer readings
and the state of the wind
were noted on the slate

the sea inverted,
tiny,
on the back of the stilled lens

the lamp was cleaned
the fountain full
blinds on the window etc.

glass washed free of salt
gleams, glints, polished brass
white paint, order

the outside doors closed
the clock stopped, no fire lit
looking into bedrooms, the beds empty

a dazzle of sun on the lens
the homely smell of paraffin
guano, weed, wind

— had his seaboots and oilskins on
— also his seaboots on, only an old waterproof coat, and that is away
— his wearing coat left behind him, out in shirt sleeves

(night coming on
we could not stay
as to make something of their fate)

Source: Northern Lighthouse Board

TRADITIONAL EXPLANATION FOR A MODERN TRAGEDY

They were strangers to the place, hadn't understood
the wave formation; maybe hadn't known
they must not speak the island's name

– except to call it *Country*.
And maybe no one had told them not to say
rock, but *hard*; not *slippery*, but *soft*.

Maybe they'd eased nature where the boat lay;
or maybe – their feet first touching fresh turf – they'd failed
to uncover their heads and turn sunways.

Maybe they'd killed a fowl before prayers
or maybe they'd missed the prayer of thanksgiving
or prayers for the morning, or vespers –

for The Country is a place of great sanctity
and knows it own, and *inconveniences ensue*
after transgressions of the least nicety.

Source: Martin Martin: *A Description of the Western Islands of Scotland*, 1716

A LEWIS CHESS PIECE, HER GRIEVANCE

Aawok he will say to make me smile,
and snort when they come in the morning
to brush salt from the baize.

It is not of a colour I like. We should have blues,
the deep blue of an ocean in sun, or pale
from the ice melt. It is always too hot here.

Aawok he'll grunt, close in the night
and we'll speak of how light castles
underwater, the sweetness of clams.

They sent a sister queen away with two knights.
The world is everywhere the same, she says,
returned. We drain our horn cups.

Aawok, my king roars, raising his sword:
remember our little house among the dunes,
tides pulsing, stories we begin to forget.

Such thrones. Such crowns. And still
my hand is to my cheek in horror
as I stare through time with salt eyes.

Aawok sounds in the bone we are.
They touch us with soft gloves.
Their reverence is killing us.

ON RE-READING *TÌR A' MHURAIN*

Paul Strand's photographs of S.Uist, 1954

Tripod legs deep in the sand a quarter-century later
to photograph what could have been the same
cursive lengths of thongweed, I wondered
how he had coped with the wind. Maybe like me
he'd strapped his camera-bag underneath,
a drogue against the weight of air on his bellows,
the dark cloth over his shoulders a sail
he had to sheet-in to shade his ground glass.

They say he'd wait hours for the light,
give people days to forget about the camera,
days running into months and becoming timeless
on the page: *Seascape, Portrait, Window, Window,*
Landscape, Portrait, Doorway – photographs
that draw us over thresholds and expose us
to faces which gaze directly at us, knowing
we shall never know tenacity like theirs.

To call the walling *rubble* would be to miss its foursquare
endurance. The roof had gone. The doorway held,
stone and lichen constant across the years.
I could see hints of white paint still on the ingo
but no trace of the inner wall patterned with rosebuds
oddly – printed in black and white – like paw-prints
behind walking stick, crook and shovel.
I photographed the granite as an abstract.

He photographed a boy leaning on the wall,
shirt too big and short itchy trousers cut from homespun,
a boy born the same year as me and taught
in the same language – which has no words
for his experience of the world: *Machair. Clachan.*

Barefoot, the boy slings his jacket over one shoulder
and grasps a stick, like the shepherd he might be
now – if he survived, – if he stayed.

I could have shown the portrait to the man
who slowed his pick-up to watch me focussing,
nodded, and drove on. *Do you remember this boy?*
It was not so many years ago, I could have asked
showing him the book, *the American with a wooden camera?*
But I knew by heart the page that says *old wrongs*
seem far from righted and stood waiting for the sky
to alter shadows in the strandline's wrack and bone.

THE PEREGRINATIONS OF
LOPHIUS PISCATORIUS   *monkfish*

Not just sand, he's down there
in a hollow, motionless
and waiting for a ripple
to excite the water.
He exhales more slowly –
here comes a saithe, nosy and near.
He waggles his lure   *illicium*

Glop. Sand settles round him.
You don't see the saithe?
Watch: here comes a Norway pout   *dominant species in stomach analyses*
Slow exhalation: he waggles his lure
Glop, sand settles, no pout.
0.72 seconds.
Haddock? *Glop*, no haddock.

A pull in the tide,
a little shimmy with his tail
and he's lifting away north
singing to the moon *Glunta, Glunta*   *moon (Shetlandic tabu word)*
mak hit kaam, mak wis fast.
Tide turns, he drops,
sand settles, *Glop*

and so he goes, doing the S T S T   *Selective Tidal Stream Transport*
Glunta owre aa
one thousand and seventy-eight days
of glop and settle ahead of him
until – eight items already in his stomach –
his eyes fix a cod.
He waggles his lure

two cod, he opens wide,
five, a crush   a tearing along
the pressure   gaping for water
pain in his gills   racket in ear stones

     the   scorching   screeching   air

Hey Jimmy, we got a [   ] here   *expletive omitted*
wi' a [   ] yellow tag on him.   *expletive omitted*

AN UNSPOKEN RULE ABOUT DISTANCES

This is a new sea, grey and steep-to:
the shore plunges and defeats the waves
– all they ever intended, they say
was to fiddle with the little stones like this, like this.

Figures appear, bundled and wrapped.
They crouch, secretive,
set up small tents and shelters
busy themselves with lamps and primuses.

Yellow loom from their storm lanterns
parcels out the long straight shore and hastens the night
– in a film the scene would shift now, focus
on a figure bent making tea, say, or attending a rod –

but two slow hours of sink and skid along the shingle,
an ache at the back of the knee
the temperature touching zero
and as far as you can see dim lamps glow at intervals

apart enough that a voice won't carry.
Theirs are solitary acts:
walk all night and they'll continue,
these silent privacies of concentration.

Most hunch in their little shelters, stare out
where they've cast at a shimmer of moon.
In large white letters, the credits: THIS IS ENGLAND;
this is the place I was born to; how little I know.

ONE NINE SIX

He sways forward and back in his chair
re-living how he tried to counteract the roll
before turning aft to see what the helm was up to
– twenty, fifty, no a hundred yards behind

but in the water, with a broken tiller in her hand.
My own memories of being catapulted out
when the laminated timber sprang apart,
of being rescued, being towed, and wet and cold

are – after all these years – submerged in his:
I don't picture the boat sailing on without me,
my father unaware and trying to steady her;
I see myself a distant head and brandishing a spar,

I feel the rudderless boat slewing up to wind
broaching then tipping over, and endure
his dread, his mix of disappointment and relief
in the sudden quiet when she wallows.

He sold that boat when I left home. Narrow and racy
she was a teenager's dream, not a fifty-year-old's.
196? On the Mersey someone said, years ago.
She must be long gone now, rotted or smashed.

We didn't keep faith with that boat, though his memory
does – one of his favourite tales. The punch line
comes with a thump on his chair: *All the same
we won the cup.* So we did, Dad, so we did.

MEMORY'S BICYCLES

I can remember the exact shade of pink
and how *Pink Witch* was painted on both sides
of the frame. I'd tell you I loved that bike
but the photos show me smiling and proud
of a bike that is black – a Raleigh
with straight handlebars. Why wasn't it pink?
I ask my father to tell me about that time –
This one's outside Joe Briscoe's: did we live there?
did I have friends? I wasn't much more than a child
I say, but he says I'll remember better than him.

It's not that he forgets – he'd have been in his forties,
a decade when memory's seen it before
and isn't laying much down. What's more vivid
is leaving school at fifteen, pay packets
and being apprenticed – and he's clear
about how many hours ahead of high tide
he stood on the wharf and how anxious he felt
watching Billyboys sail over from Hull
the day his father had promised a bike.

Such longing for a bike – *that* I can believe,
though no one was there *(Watch the birdie!)* with a camera,
so you have to imagine it lifted from the hold
and manhandled down to a boy on the dockside
telling his young brothers *Don't touch!*
And if you could pedal to Dragonby Hill
before the bus, and grab the handle at the back
and the driver didn't see, you could get a pull
right to the top. So maybe his bike's believable too.
Unless that were some other boy behind the bus.

LOST

Turning off the M1 because
there are little back roads that go straight there
un-numbered or not even on the map.

And no landmarks – this is flat country.
Yet another crossroads
and you're guessing which way's east.

Now and again the name of a pit,
not making a map
but an echo of talk long ago.

A fingerpost backwards, or the same whichever road,
and all of it equally unknown –
late in the day and feeling like a good cry

then stopping to ask. *That way, love,* they say.
Now you have a stranger's accent
you hear it kindly said: *Keep going, love.*

✳

A dual carriageway speeding you on,
and craning backwards for the street names
There! but on the other side, across the barrier

and all the changes (those PVC doors) exactly what you'd expect
– only the cemetery stones below the flyover
smoke-black still,

the weight of what's beyond reach
bearing down, not just place
after all, but self.

DUSTING BOOKSHELVES, I TAKE DOWN
SHADOW OF LIGHT

The view from the kitchen (may blossom turned pink
by rain), loose squeal of a doorknob, clatter of bottles
into the rack – the everyday things of every day here

or a smell on the breeze (diesel, say, and brine)
one day when you knew you were happy:
no way of storing them. No way to remember –

albums filled with weddings and parties
nearly as untypical as remembering
an eggcup from one house, grate from another.

Only a photographer like Brandt, so light on his feet
as not to disturb even the air, opens a door in time
you think maybe you'd opened yourself long ago

or one just like it with its step and a bucket,
the futility of scrubbing it clean, though it's all art,
the violence done to shades of grey by black and white.

In a journal I wrote when I lived in L.A., Blalock's
out on the lawn. Who was Blalock? What was he like?
Him, and all those others I was so sure I'd recall.

SO HOW MUCH IS INVENTION?

Another letter to Charles Wright

Autobiography amazes me:
                        how did you get it right, Charles,
grasses bright and erect at Desenzano
some forty-five years ago?

It can't be a matter of notebooks and journals:
I've no faces for names in the book of my own time abroad;
I'd need a map to tell you where Obispo is.

All I'm left with is the journey back –
black tea and horizons my cure for seasickness,
a ship's blanket on a metal deck, the smell of wet paint,

evenings lengthening further north, and suns
setting all the colours through peach into night
– not of the new world nor of the old
                           but the ocean between

each wave insisting on a present tense
I thought I could be happy in forever,
freed from demands and expectations. Cut

to dockside faces looking up, tiny
                       and expectant,
Roberto seeing them before I did.
(Had I shown him a photo? Were they holding a sign?)

I remember getting off to a bad start they didn't forgive:
Looks so small I said (semis, roads, the black Rover 90) meaning
I couldn't believe how tricksy memory could be

and still can't,
                     knowing whatever *grasses bright and erect*
I trampled today won't surface again,
memory's camera not even unpacked for ordinary days.

AUTOBIOGRAPHY

Million Women Survey 2009/10

When I was ten I lived in a house with an indoor toilet
and slept alone. I've never worked nights,
never been a hairdresser, a flight attendant or a cook.
It's a long time since I was questioned about sex,
children even, and other wounds. Dark, very dark:
no holidays in sunny places.
I talk to no one on a mobile phone.

Every day I duck out of cycling home and heavy lifting,
avoid talcum powder, sunbeds and mouthwash
but do have bowel movements and deodorant
and eat two tablespoons of uncooked tomatoes.
(This is about lycopene: the tablespoon's large.)
I don't sleep much; the early hours are full of ghosts.
Every day, slow average brisk brisk brisk.

Hazel – glasses on, my eyesight's good
though without them landscape's more mysterious
and creatures skulk in every shadow.
I'm as tall as I was in my twenties,
but drink more. Hard to say whether
I've fewer freckles than other women –
I asked Sheila in the Post Office this afternoon.

Warm, hot, getting very hot. I had a fall.
Some things are worse than broken bones.
I'm always asked about my blood relations.
Yes, yes, yes, yes, yes, yes, yes: all those genes
are stacked against me. Yes, I've had the tests
and all the same, would say that I am happy
slightly moderately deeply (tick) uniquely.

THINK OF US AS WE WERE

Send an old photo, I'd like that
he writes. To remember us by

as we were before telephones, mortgages,
the weekday half-mile for the 8.30 bus

and I've found one, the two of us
at the top of some steps, turning –

someone must have shouted to us *Wait*:
we're turning together, front feet

mid-step in a two-step
arms swinging out and laughing

bearded and long-haired
such beautiful people so sixties

dancing, as the camera has it
of that half-turn half-backward glance

over the shoulder at us,
the people they did not become.

Don't look for a storyline;
don't ask where they went,

I like them there on the top step
feet not quite touching the ground

step two and turn   step step and glide,
the afternoon sunlight unshadowed and kind.

A DAY'S WORK

World comes knocking. *NO!* –
easy as that, when it's the darkroom door.

Not the dark of endings, of night, of fear:
this is the dark of beginnings

an orderly dark you know
your way round in, scissors here, pencil there

a dark you're as at home in
as if you could see the notes you write.

Only water flows here; time's
stopped by a button on a clock with no hours

– then allowed little increments:
seven-and-a-half minutes for film, three for paper;

you know the ticks by heart.
Stopped again. Silence.

It is possible not to think: it is possible
to sit on a high stool at the sink

nothing but a hand, its gentle rocking
of sheet film in a dish; stop, fix.

Here are the pleasures of precision:
metol 8 grams, water at 40 degrees;

here you believe in the idea of perfection
approached with little rituals to slow the pulse.

A third print comes closest.
There have been times I've tried a fifth.

Beautiful, the deep wet blacks
and silver highlights tailing towards invisible,

the print never quite so heartfelt
in the light. O world,

all day turning without me.
Back in your noisy brightness

I stand in the garden like an amnesiac,
unable to account for how it comes to be evening.

ELEGY FOR MY METERS

Cloudy-bright they were called in the small print
enclosed with every film. Cloudy-bright days,
the easy ones, landscapes lying open,
nothing harsh in the sunlight, nothing hidden by shade.
Did we really need meters?

We bought them, calibrated and compared them.
We metered the shine on smooth rock,
leaves rotting under trees, cloud in a pool.
We made notes and allowances and calculations,
could use the back of our hand for Zone VI

and as I remember somehow my answer
– stopped right down – was always 2.
I think we used them for the joy of performance;
I think they were part of a ritual to delay
that moment of commitment with the shutter

though in front of the tripod and inside the picture
we regarded the needle and its certainties
as reverently as if it registered *soul*
– which it did in a way, the feel of a place
what we believed we were after, not just the look.

You should watch where you're putting your feet
you said this morning when I fell on the hill.
I'd been looking at mist in the valley
– every droplet refracting thin sun –
and printing the distances ahead impossibly bright.

The weather's changed now, darkest shadows
under the alder at the edge of the wood, highlights
on tufted hair grass streaming downwind.
The meter in the pocket camera I carry with me
broke years ago. A cloudy-bright day, *f*11.

LIGHT READINGS AT KEILDER

i.m. M. J.

It was the trees you were drawn to, printing them
black into black as if you dared yourself on paper
like you'd dare yourself further into forests.

The reservoir's almost natural now;
some hillsides clearfelled.
No one seems to pick wild raspberries these days.

Still, no one puts their hands
in trays of metol either, making prints.
There was talk about the chemicals when you died.

Now I'm here, I'd say it was the darkness
you took in through your skin
though I remember you better for the light:

halfway across the estuary mudflats at low tide
– that was dangerous, you know –
answering simply by lifting your dark cloth

to show me on the ground glass (small hands for a man)
how light could riff on nothing,
so not once since have I thought there's nothing

to see. Late again now, reading cloud shadow
against shade at the edge of the trees, and nothing
to show for the day but a handful of fruits,
wind turning wild raspberry leaves silver side up.

THEY VISIT THEIR DEAD

Out here it's June before the long straight hedgerows
clot with may. What my father calls kesh
foams on the verge. I don't remember, he says,
the lanes as narrow when I was biking to school.

It's Sunday. The church is locked and no service
till next month; the graveyard's abandoned –
it's hopeless. We wade in anyway, arms up,
nettles and grasses chest high, having to feel

for the humps and hollows of plots with our feet;
now and again pull ivy and grass from a stone.
I'm stung through my clothes. It's comical really,
his white head disappeared among cow parsley umbels.

We'd need a billhook and scythe, and a week.
It takes the two of us to shut the gate. We lean on it, quiet.
I'm thinking how everyone left the village (like him)
and none of the offcomers would know any names

when he says: that's why it's best to be scattered.
We've had this argument before: the pollution card wins
but I leave it unplayed: it's his birthday – he's 90
and we both know he is also talking about himself.

The way the wind smooths the seedheads and grasses,
you'd think it was the ancestors turned their backs
on us and our profligate ways, and wilfully cloaked themselves
with cocksfoot and catstail, burdock and brome.

BUCOLIC (1960-2010)

1960's

All the men drinking beer.
His father going out into the night,
returning with a pint-pot:

the milk thick, sweet and still warm.
— *Get this across you Lass,*
put some flesh on those bones.

1970's

— *Can you send your Jane?*
It's urgent:
I need someone with small hands.

The field by the cattle grid.
A torch. — *I'll hold her.*
Put your arm in, feel for the legs.

The ground all mud and squelch.
A thin snow blowing about.
A feed sack round his shoulders.

— *What did he want, Dear?*
(Soap and hot water, more soap.)
— *Oh just something   he couldn't reach.*

1980's

Flies. The sway of full bags
on the slow walk from river to parlour.
Drips of milk   all the way home.

His dog's come with me,
her eyes sad with reproach:
I'm not doing this right.

Every day of his life, except this one.
Even so – *You took your time.*
Every cow her own place. Every day.

1990's

The thin blue smoke of his vented temper
among the scrub. Sudden flares
and bursts of red sparks.

Nothing is ever said about this.
All year long, gaunt and blackened whin
shows kissing's (clearly) not in season.

2000's

Between us now a "Wildlife Corridor",
new fence and five-bar gate
–That'll see us both out.

Classic: elbows on the top rail,
a blade of grass, eyes missing nothing.
Hands twice the width of mine.

*Pays more to grow weeds and wildflowers
these days than milk cows.
You'll keep an eye on things while I'm away?*

Such few things: grass growing
in the concrete yard; what time the first bat
strikes out from the old milking parlour at dusk.

RABBIT HOLE

I knew where it started, but not where it ended.
Nests up to two metres in the books say.
I'd expected to find the place where cruelty
lies low in us all, but this was easy:

poking a cane into the potato patch
after all these dry weeks, the tunnel fell in.
In dust at the end, potatoes,
movement. A leg, feet and claws,

a burrowing down and a stillness
as of held breath. I changed my mind –
not about the act, but the method.
Fetched a full bucket.

One by one, part-furred, still blind.
Eyes open at about 7 days.
I was quick and efficient: five pale pink mouths.
And thorough. Dug down. Six.

Their only moment in the light.
My pulse rate never changed.
Then I dug a trench by the raspberries
and laid them in a neat row. Soil like dust.

The nest-lining of summer-scented hay
and belly fur went to the compost.
You didn't look at me when you asked – *OK?*
– *Mm*, I said, *Soil was loose after all these dry weeks.*

EQUINOCTIAL BLUES

Autumn again. Twisting the apples
to see if they're ripe – not yet, not yet.
A few last swallows grazing at sixty feet.
Seeip and *chakchack* in the hedgerows – the first
redwings and fieldfares on passage
across distances shiny with dew.

Well that's all as it should be
– though not this shindig of tractors
in every direction, cutting and carting
for silage clamps still empty
after a summer of rain, engines girning
long after we've gone to bed.

84 was worse Frank says *grass gone over
and re-rooted, then coming off in ropes:
there's a photo of us holding one up, 40 foot.*
"Worse in 84" – as if that might harness
these last wet months back
into the to-and-fro of some natural cycle

so all the old saws can be relied on
to predict the weather and work.
But when did we last hear a cuckoo?
– one year the valley playing its usual tricks
with those calls, the next year
not.

OCTOBER SUN, BLUE SKY AND
YELLOW LEAVES

All this choice and free will. Though I don't remember
choosing this afternoon, don't remember choosing to count
late butterflies (Red admirals, a pair of Speckled woods, one Comma),
blackbirds gobbling soft berries on the yew,
transatlantic contrails with their elbow-turns east.

The question of how to spend the rest of your life
lies low, waiting for you when you're alone.
Not much chance for it to speak out today,
tractor racket across the valley, clatter of hedge-flail here
and mackerel warnings coasting in from the west.

Nine late swallows feeding low above the roof,
coal-tits stripping pine cones near the house,
litter of scales falling as fast as forgotten days.
I can never believe I'll encounter something rare,
but sometimes I do. Sometimes, I do.

THE PRIVATE LIFE OF *LEPUS LEPUS*

i) *at his toilet*

If he had not been so particular…

the meadow still, morning light in the dew
Nothing moves
a black⠀⠀flickering

something about his left ear
he scratches scratches scratches
with his hind leg

a quick change of sides,
right leg behind right ear to even things up
then flicking the left again and again

He sits up

Paddles his front feet in the dew
rubs them together, rubs and rubs
then washes his face

Paddles in the dew
rubs his paws together and together
and washes his face

Did I see him spit on his hands?

ii) *sleeping*

Only because I already knew…

there: in the slight south-facing dip
before the meadow curves down to the wood

that last molehill in the run,
the soil slightly lighter (ears flat-packed along his back)

Day after day in his form
blades of grass just so

Is he dead?
Watch

sometimes a deep breath
– the molehill heaves

Day after day
I watch at the upstairs window

iii) about his business

Hare gone dandying
down in the woods
His fields, not mine

I can see where he lay

O I want to walk out
in his field
and touch his form

I know every blade
could walk straight there
three paces left of those rushes

iv) betrayed

After the gale, making notes:
which trees to be felled, fences
to be tightened, and a short cut

unintended
close by his form
its deep slot, angle of thigh

Old man hare lolloping by
along the berm
treats me to his disregard

He saw me
              looking
Won't be back

DECEMBER DARK DAYS

Winter at a stroke,
the lingering bronze of a lazy autumn stripped
by a night's gale. Dishevelled nets of rain
snag on the valley in greys and darker greys,
the wood across the river underexposed, a hint of itself.

To live here is to live in two landscapes:
one that needs a bank rebuilt above the watergate,
that wrenches shoulders and breaks fingernails, that's mud
hosed off boots as the light fades at the end of a day planting trees;
the other I spend so much time watching,
never quite able to grasp what it means.
                              No answers this afternoon,

the wooded slope across the river withdrawn,
a landscape sketch in greys and darker greys.
A single gale, and dishevelled nets of rain
drag under the colours and ease of autumn.
Winter at a stroke.

SALVAGE JOB, HE SAID, *THIS HEDGE OF YOURS*

When I get back with the tea,
               old rails and thorns are heaped in the field,
                      three liggers already laid low on the cop.

He's tender with it, the axe
               working behind the bark with his right,
                      his left hand coaxing a stem till it creaks,

the lightest of taps, another inch of caress,
               a small groan and the stiff old thornbush
                      compliant as when it was a whip.

He looks at the knot of roots and thick stems
               and says strange thing is, he can hear
                      his Old Man telling him which to take out,

how to dig round a bole
               and swivel the stock
                      on the hold of a single good root

– he wouldn't have thought
               he'd been listening, his mind as a lad
                      always on Fridays and the Floral Hall.

When I get back with more stakes,
               he says *It's come back to me now,*
                      you'll like this, it's a geb

so I write in my pocket book *geb (hard G)*
               and sit drawing the crook-shape
                      he cut from an angle of trunk and drove into the cop

to clamp springy lengths inwards and down –
      there being no word I can think of
           to explain what it does.

Soon be cowing-up time, I say,
      giving him back the word on my previous page
           – a word, it says not just (underlined) about milking

but straw for the calves,
      a handful of grain for the hens,
           gathering in tools at the end of a day –

Looks fine to me,
      but the Old Man's having a field day today,
           out of his grave again and elbowing between us

to stab at the hedge with the stem of his pipe
      telling us – like they say he always did
           when it came to judging competitions –

No good going by how it looks, fresh laid;
      what it's like come July
           is what counts.

THE BLACK HEIFER

Every morning a black heifer scrambles
through my neighbour's fence. He's blocked the gap
with a pallet, with broken rails, binder twine and a wardrobe door
and still she comes. This is what she does,

while my geese graze east of the house.
They flow from one meadow to the next
predictable as tides. What time is it?
Not yet four, they're not yet back from the pond.

My father, too. Whatever the weather
he fetches his paper at nine. This
is what he does. This is how we shape
the days, sameness speeding them up.

As for me, I stand at the window just before eight,
watch a small black cow shrug off rusty wire, and say
I'll sell up and move on. A new place every day
will slow things down. Any day now.

AGAINST SPRING

We've seen it all before,
sunlight revamped by tender green
not yet leaf, how you wake one morning
to blossoms everywhere then petals
are everywhere and scents and pollen
and the upsurge of bluebells quick
before the canopy thickens, and I say

give me back the bones, give me
the spare forms of winter, its necessity.
Let me look out on grey, its subtleties.
My life, too: just enough plain bowls
and no more, for those who want soup.
My parents, visiting, unpack a box saying
you should have this, we have no need.

Once as a child I was sent with sweet williams
for the old man next door. The vase
was where he said, middle shelf
– one of those floor-to-ceiling cupboards
from the fifties with sliding doors –
along from the cups. There were three,
a pile of newspapers and empty shelves.

Even mementoes we once thought to keep
are lost on the way. How little in the end
we want: at the edge of the shore
mowed grass, yellow lichen on stone.

FIELD NOTES

We had talked the evening into bat-light
when he gestured with his eyes *Turn; look*.
A tawny – flat face against the glass, balanced
on the sill, wings (arms, I almost said) outspread.
Maybe it was a far glow from the kitchen
across indoor plants and wooden stairs drew the owl
as to a roost. An arm's-length from where we sat.

It is not true they only hunt at night.
The year they were calling from each end of the garden
I saw one slide from view behind the hedge
at noon. And once, blackbird commotions
made me run into the Little Wood: two paces in
an owl dropped the henbird at my feet.
Alive but too ripped and bloodied to save.

The owl kept up its slow beat at the pane.
Quiet as we could, still urgent, we talked on
and I thought that if I had been the friend
sitting by me, I would have been stricken:
the light gone, the great bird glaring down,
him saying *I've caused that much pain*
and not knowing how to stop.

THE TEACHINGS OF *STRIX ALUCO*

First you must learn stillness.
You must learn to wait inside shadow:
even your breath must not disturb
the air around you. Forget time. Forget
the body – be nothing but eyes:
a last blackbird fruitless on the lawn,
a pair of rooks giving up on the day
as day gives itself up to the night.

Clear your mind of shades of grey.
Dusk is not, as you think, continuum.
There is a moment when it is day; after it, night.
You will learn this is not the same as when electric lights
click on in the milking parlour across the valley. No,
night comes always later than you expect.
Study the light. Make a judgment of your own:
this is your second lesson.

Watch.   Watch.
If you have judged right,
out of the fold in the cypress tree,
out of that cleft between day and night
in one swift unfolding downward swoop,
                    I:
one wingbeat and your world is dark.
Watch.   Watch as well as you can and you will lose me.
You will never be able to say where I went, what I do.
This is the lesson you won't ever learn:
how much there is you can never know.

SEXING THE WOODPECKER

Black nape – female you say, passing the binoculars
and doubling the garden's population. She's flown
before I've sketched the pattern on her tail.

Years ago, on the way to work, Don said
Take the hill road; look: temperature inversion –
you've the perfect valley for these fogs.

There's always so much more to find out.
No river runs straight more than ten times
its width. The uplift one wingbeat

gives to another. Turbulence generates eddies.
Random's an idea that's useful
only when you've no interest in the world.

I wish my neighbour would stop telling me
why she wants to kill her husband.
It's a different reason every week.

A CHANGEABLE ANSWER

Monday for the cessation of rain, for sharp wind
on the moor – a Möbius twist of starlings
so far from a roost they're out to practise
their loops & stalls, & mine the only applause;

last Tuesday for the sound of the river
& its sun-glint through trees, windblows
logged and brashed, the many hands,
the cups of tea, the world set to rights;

or Wednesday for the gold flare late in the west
& a sudden drift of rime from clear sky
hung across middle-distance
like tracing paper half-masking the view;

or Thursday for frost & hard ground
melt-shadows in sun, red flames on clean logs
cut from dead elm & the field-away
tap of posts driven in for a fence;

then Friday for nothing beyond the hedge,
a monochrome garden in unforecast fog,
sun through a slit like a lightbulb, then suddenly not,
fog regrouping to bandage the river downstream;

yesterday for enough breeze to hang washing on,
rain holding off, grey clouds relenting
for a peaches-and-cream finale
before evening's last rinse in deep mauve;

& today for wind made visible
by processions of drizzle, so mild again
lacewings litter the house – one's here,
on the keyboard, an iridescence on **Q** –

any of them, any: I don't care which;
even tomorrow with its forecast for storm.

THE FIELD OF MIRACLE

We were not there and it was nothing
to do with us but like the man who ran
on to the platform just as the doors hissed shut
and those who'd got off three minutes before,
we were awake in the night imagining
the noise, the darkness and might-have-beens,
because we had been there so many evenings
at dusk in that quiet dip between fells, to watch
starlings – thirty thousand or so – streak in close,
swirl and swarm into a single miraculous
being of the skies as they gathered to roost.
And none of the people clambering
from the metal and glass on to the muddy field
to whisper *miracle* at the feel of light rain
on their faces could have known theirs
was the second that day, the birds nearby
folded safe in a small stand of spruce.
And *miracle* was the newreaders' word
telling us be glad, as if it were something
to do with us, only one person killed
and she in her eighties – as if that made it
a lesser death, when maybe we should think it
greater, all that lost experience,
her hoard of days from inside history
– the thirty thousand or so she'd gathered – gone,
gone like the starlings after that night of voices,
that long night of sirens and arc-lamps and rotors,
only a certain absence murmuring where they'd been.

NINE STRAWBERRIES

She's asleep.

Dreaming,
         she smiles
then waves – the long slow wave you'd wave
wanting to stand out on the platform
                          as the train pulls away.

I wait until the clank of pistons dies down
and the train's just a cloud of steam down the line:

Hello, I say, fancy finding you here.
She cries of course.

Not knowing the rules, instead of flowers
I've brought her a last few hothouse fruits.

Here's the most perfect: scarlet and heart-shaped.
It goes in whole,
               thirst-quenching, and she's smiling again:

My first strawberry of the season, she says.
Why contradict? I pick off the calyx and pass her
another first strawberry of the season.

Berry after berry passes between us,
each of them a surprise, delicious.
She has never been so easy to please.

Ten minutes of the slow October afternoon pass
in pure pleasure.
                  It doesn't last:
before I've wiped the spot of juice from her chin,

it's beyond recall. It cannot be savoured
– in a moment she'll ask what the empty punnet's for –
can't be recounted to the next one who visits,
will not comfort the loneliness of night,

as irretrievable as whoever it was
leaning from the open window of the train,

                                        smaller and smaller

towards the vanishing point.

I REMEMBER THE IMPULSE TO DRAW

I remember thinking none of it
would stay with me, the pattern
of roads and rooftops below, car parks
emptying, filling up and emptying again,
the rattle of a metal trolley and voices
calling along the corridor.
How it made you long for quiet.

I'd two sketchbooks in my bag,
several pencils. Even Indian ink.
I could see how I'd make the one line flow
with a single movement, elbow through wrist.
I remember thinking my hand
wouldn't falter, that line was so clear
all this time keeping watch.

I could even feel the way paper's
warm under the hand.
I knew it so well now, I thought,
the weight of the head falling back,
the line of brow – nose – lip
above the gape of small breaths,
I'd be able to draw it later. Anytime.

The largest sheet I have, thick and off-white.
All morning at the drawing board
remembering the impulse to draw –
and nothing.
As if black-gloved hands are held tight
over an inner eye, memory saying
Not this. No.

WINGS

A goose hates to be touched,
         every feather alive
and held just so, wing-tips over the tail.

Even from a field away, it's how you know
         a goose is dead
– the way its wings splay down.

Gathering the corpse, feathers
         have a used-up feel.
The neck hangs loose.

When flight's gone
         you never recognise the bird
(only the leg ring tells you – last year's gander).

*

When my mother died
         nothing changed.
Her skin was soft.

The in-and-out of little breaths
         must have stopped
but I couldn't say exactly when.

Whatever it is can be said
         to *leave* the body
flew off on invisible wings.

Later – when my father asked me for her necklace –
         I heard myself apologise,
the weight of her head in my hand, the pillow warm.

A COLD DAY, AFTER ALL THAT SUN

Setting down a bowl of soup and hearing
her voice, *I have a weakness for white bowls made
to be good in the hands* and wondering
what was it she was really telling you –
would that memory didn't do this.

I wish memory were the outbarn this morning,
shelter from the squall that ripped new leaves
and soaked me. The air inside still and familiar:
dust in the low light, old bales, stone walls
giving back the warmth of last week's sun

though sometimes there's a bar across the doors,
the bolts shot home; and sometimes what you're sure
you left there bright and polished's so pitted
when your astonished thought touches it
it crumbles into flakes that won't rebuild.

GLASSHOUSE

Soon it will smell of tomatoes,
tender herbs too if you rub their leaves
and a foxy pelargonium, the old-fashioned sort,
but for now it's the velvet scented refuge
of alpine auriculas. Come in again,
it's inside and outside at once: new greens
at infinity, dark petals in close up.
How perfect they are, out of the weather,
meal on their stems. They don't last long.
Aren't you surprised how warm it is,
how a sheet of thin glass keeps out the wind?
A membrane that thin round our lives:
a rabbit startling the car into a swerve;
a life-line only seeming clipped-on
and the next wave bearing the body away.
A pane breaks, one unruly cell, and all the order
of pots and blooms we were counting on's gone.

FORTUNE

I love slipping from the bed to the silence of the kitchen
in the nearly-dark of winter mornings, sitting at the table
with a teacup in my hands – always the same one,
an old chip opposite the handle – and watching skies:
rosy dapples fading over Cowkins or today's
something-and-nothing of a lit edge beyond Helks,
but mostly greys, these slowly lifting shades of grey.

You come in, flip the switch, floods of yellow light.
I love this too, your turning the page on the calendar
and reading the day's poem aloud – *Read it again,*
that bit about fortune and earthly things –
and the talk after. I love them both: the silence
and your voice reading; the yellow brightness
and the greys out there thrown suddenly to purple.

Then there is more tea and more talk and the earthly things
have assumed their daylight raiment and though at times
it still comes to mind, I have not used the word *tomorrow*.

HEADED FOR THE COAST

He gave me a small blue box
to shut my pain in, the sort
a child might keep a mouse in
with a finger hole and sliding lid.
My pain is bigger than a mouse.

He made me a transparent ramp
to herd my pain into a sheep-trailer.
My pain is as stupid as a sheep
and will not be driven; it stares,
malevolence in its yellow eyes.

He lent me his bicycle and the coat
he bought on Skipton market
but I hurt too much
to pedal away from my pain.
I've kept the coat – set out on foot.

Fish-hooks in its pocket –
a type I've not come across before:
I'm headed for the coast.
On Muckle Flugga I'll unravel
the old coat's raggy hem to spin a line –

I'm going to fish up an island
from the sea-bed, a new place
where pain can't put down roots.
I'll be gone for the usual time,
a year and a day. And so goodbye.